THE DAYS I DREAM OF

Second Edition

3 5 7 9 10 8 6 4

Saint John's, Antigua
West Indies

First printed in December 2021

Images from Canva ©

Visit the author's website at
https://lmsanguinette.wordpress.com

DEDICATION

This small book of poems is dedicated to the dreamers of the world, to the friends I've gained along the way, and to those who time has taken.

"Sometimes, it's nice to have our pain seen. Other times, all we desire is hope for the better days."
~L. M. Sanguinette

THE DAYS I DREAM OF

A COLLECTION OF POEMS

L. M. Sanguinette

CONTENTS

ACKNOWLEDGMENTS

As my introduction into the world of publishing, it would be remiss of me not to thank those people who have assisted in the process of turning a dream into a reality. Firstly, I'd like to thank the two editors whose trained eyes offered insight into areas in which the poems needed improvement, Anya Jimenez, and Cara Flannery.

Next, I'd like to thank my family, who have always supported me and my various—sometimes outlandish—choices in life. Most of them are still unaware that they are mentioned in these books, and I'm sure a handful of them are unaware these books exist.

Finally, I'd like to thank my friends who not only inspired many of these poems but have helped me become the person I am today, allowing me to grow, and seeing the beauty in my messy mind, even and especially when I didn't see myself.

INTRODUCTION

This book is a collection of poems and reflections born from deep introspection and self-discovery. It is an amalgamation of thoughts that surfaced during moments of personal struggle, where I sought solace through writing. However, it is not a book solely about darkness and despair, as it also explores moments of joy and lightness that we experience in life.

The poems within cover a diverse range of topics, from simple everyday pleasures like sipping on a cup of coffee, to grappling with the complexities of grief and loss. They offer insightful commentaries on life's challenges and provide a means of reflection for those seeking a deeper understanding of their own experiences.

BEGINNINGS

Beginnings are beautiful things. Sometimes, they mean the promise of something new. The journey into the unknown. *The first.*

Other times, they are simply the grand opening to a previous close. The chance to start afresh. Not the journey into the unknown but the new transition into an already known.

Many beginnings we take for granted, like that of daybreak or the first page of a book, even–and almost especially–that first sip of coffee in the morning. These beginnings, these crucial moments, mark the way you react to whatever is to come next.

CAFÉ LATTE

Made with espresso, steamed milk, and milk foam, the Café Latte, or Latte for short, is the quintessential breakfast drink. For those who need a large pick me up before starting their day or simply wish to indulge in something rich and decadent, this coffee has you covered.

In Italy, customs state you are only allowed to have milk in coffee at the start of your day, which makes it the perfect drink to kick off our story. Luckily, poetry doesn't abide by such strict protocol.

The following poems take on warm, welcoming, and sometimes whimsical tones. Great for light introspection and easy reading. Recommended for consumption at the beginning of the day. Accompany with something sweet and pleasurable.

THIS DAY IS FOR COFFEE

this day is for coffee
for the sharp smell of beans in the morning
for that first sip of bitterness
for that shock to the system
for the sleep that lingers in my eyes

this day is for cold hands holding warm mugs
for focused inhales
and steam-cooling exhales
for those brief moments of stillness
before the world wakes

this day is for mug stains on wooden coasters
for the blissful silence
as the sunlight trickles in
filtering through my windows
to welcome me again

this day is for blank pages and unopened books
for new ink from old pens
for vivid dreams from the night before
that kept me up 'til odder hours
waiting to come to life

this day is for coffee
before the chaos creeps slowly in
so I take another sip
and let the day begin.

OPEN THE DOORS

Today I open the door to imagination,
the gates to a world I cannot comprehend
but feel the need to share on paper
and laugh about with a friend.

Today I pull back the curtain that hides
the insanity within my mind
to shine a light on the anxious thoughts
wedged in all the crevices they can find.

BE THAT SUNSHINE

Be that sunshine
the kind that twinkles in the morning's dewdrops
and plays at the gaps where my eyelids don't close
as it nudges me awake.

Be that sunshine
the kind that makes me think of summer
and smells of coconuts and salt water
even if only to me.

Be that sunshine
the kind that reminds me of the many yesterdays
when I felt helpless, whose many tomorrows
proved I was strong.

Be that sunshine
and I too will be yours, sun and moon
and sky full of stars, let shine from us a blinding light
to bathe the world in our glow.

LET IN THE DAWN

Let the dawn creep slowly over
the hillsides and the mountaintops
and spread through the valleys wide
so that it may remind us all
of what it means to be awake, alive
adrift though we may be but still
we find a way to make it work,
to guide us through the waves of life
by the light of the breaking dawn.

WALKING THE SILENT STREETS

Here I walk the silent streets
of the city that never sleeps and yet
all is quiet in the morning air
and I think to myself how lucky I am
for this brief moment of stillness before
I truly start the day.

Here I walk the silent streets
alone but never lonely am I
when the sun's rays shine beside me
and the cool breeze tugs me along
while the grass dances up to meet my feet
and the trees bend to wave hello.

MARSHMALLOWS IN MY CHOCOLATE

My little eyes had always seen
marshmallows in my hot chocolate.

Fluffy white clouds to cover the rich brown lake,
the one that tastes like heaven on earth,
and makes my little mouth water.

I watch them melt, licking their sugary foam
from my pinky plush lips, as I spy on people who
cringe at the drinks they force down their throats
without remorse.

I'd pity the image they have of themselves
which I think must be strict to stop them too
from licking chocolate off their noses.

But nowadays I look from over a smaller cup,
the one you use for bitter espresso
that makes me shiver as it touches my tongue
and I wonder when I became one of them.

SITTING IN SILENCE

My mind is a constant whirling and whirring
of gears that tick and cogs that squeak
while a bundle of buzzing bees buzz outside
away from whizzing wasps
that chase a creeping curious cat that cries
in meow to the cow that moos and munches
through the swishy scratchy scrunchy grass
that bends and blows with the busy breeze
that whistles through the swarming streets
where people's papers take to the skies
like rockets gurgling and hurling upwards
into the dark and silence of space,
when I remember I too should be silent,
in a contemplative meditation that
I am dragged from by my phone's alarm
and because of this I know for sure
I will not be still today.

PEN TO PAPER

It's time for me to start afresh
and mar this paper with my pen
to sully its blankness with scribbles that somehow
form words in one language and tales in another.

The possibilities are endless;
the empty page waits to transform
into something that maybe children will read,
of the knights on horseback that slay the damsels
while sea monsters dine with kings…

…wait, that doesn't sound right…

Maybe this page will be filled with mystery
and love tales for adults who wish to escape
from day jobs and night shifts
in favour of spaceships that wish to be real boys
and policemen who seek out the golden snitch…

…no, still not quite…

The point of the story, if I'll ever get there,
is waiting to be written down
on the page beneath my leaking pen
holding out for the storm of scribbles
that were destined to become stories…

…well, if only I put pen to paper.

LET'S FALL IN LOVE

Break down the walls I've built for myself
Let's fall in love
Chip away at my stone heart
Make it beat again, make it beat, again.

Talk to me, laugh with me, smile with me
take my hand and dance with me
Let's share our dreams and count the stars.
Let's look out on the world and wonder
not about who we once were,
but who together we will be.

Let's share a cup like we share secrets
and hug to keep each other warm
like the summer sun on island beaches
throughout the winter's bitter cold
as under blankets we nestle closer
so our hearts may beat as one.

And then, come inward with me
be silent and be still with me
Let's sit back and admire the life we built
because we fell in love
how time has aged us but our souls stay the same
Let our hearts do the talking from then on.

LONG TIME NO SEE

How long has it been?
You've changed. Have I?
Your nose is larger, your beard has come in.
Your voice is deeper…I like it though.

I don't know this person before me,
this new you you've become,
but I'd like to.
I remember we used to be good friends. Best friends.
Secret keepers and midnight whisperers.
But who is this new you standing before me?
And who am I to you?

Do you remember the days we spent
running around barefoot in the grass
and hiding out from passersby
who couldn't care that we were there?
Giggling kids that lived in worlds
beyond the one that we can see…

I'd like to ask, but I'm afraid.
Maybe we became strangers the day
we left home to follow our dreams.
Maybe you're just being polite when you say
long time no see.
Maybe you don't remember me, I think,
but you smile and pull me a chair.
Stay a while, you say, share a drink with me.

I'll have a hot chocolate, what about you?
The same? That's great!
No, my taste hasn't changed.
Yours hasn't either? What a coincidence,
I blush and look away.

Do you remember when we used to drink
hot chocolate…*All the time*, you say, and I smile…
And that one time you laughed so hard
it came out your nose?
You laugh.
I remember that laugh. It hasn't changed.
Neither has your smile, or the twinkle in your eyes.
I take a sip and leave a dot
of whipped cream on the tip of my nose
the way we used to before we grew.

Last I heard, you had a girlfriend?
You'd left for college with her.
Not anymore? Oh. I'm sorry, but you're not.
Last you heard I got a job? I did! Thanks…
No, I don't love it, but it pays the bills.
My dreams? You remember those?
I almost forgot them when I was too busy
looking to make a living than to live.
What about yours?
You're chasing them? I'm happy for you. Really.

Do I remember the rainy days,
the ones we'd spend in the mud, you ask?
I do, I grin from ear to ear,
remembering our little faces covered in gunk
and diving into the sea to get clean.

The drinks are done but we stay put,
unable to part ways after years of no news.
How's your mum? I'm so sorry.
How's mine? She's still going.
And your siblings? That's good.
I miss mine terribly.

Do you remember the camping trips?
Mosquitos and sand in our beds?
Staying up late to count the stars,
and even later to watch the sun.
You do? Me too…

Do I remember the race to school,
getting just in time to be not so late
and the laughs we'd share at recess
because you'd beat me that time,
but I'd get you the next?
How could I forget?
I remember more of you
than of what I learned in school,
I think but the words hang on my tongue.

Somehow we reach the doors of our cars,
keys in hand as we stand in wait
neither wanting to leave
though our new lives pull us away.

Where did the time go? you ask and stare back
at the cafe where we found our pasts again,
even if only for a moment.
Time flies–
when you're having fun, you interrupt
and we share a last laugh.

One final hug before we go
you tell me not to be a stranger and I say the same,
hoping that the next time won't be too far from now
and the next 'hi' will be a 'there you are, again'
instead of a 'long time no see'…

CAPPUCCINO

One of the more popular drinks on the menu, a cappuccino is usually equal parts espresso, steamed milk, and milk foam, and is the perfect blend of creamy and bold.

This classic Italian coffee is not just a beverage, but an art form. The frothy top, traditionally dusted with cocoa powder, creates a canvas for baristas to showcase their skills. A beverage made for creatives by creatives.

The following poems, like their creative coffee counterpart, take on a range of tones, from introspective to playful, making them a perfect companion for your midday break or evening indulgence. Sip slowly and savor the rich flavors, and let the words transport you to new realms of imagination.

POETRY

These words
so small
so few
and yet

they are given
the entire page
and stranger still
it doesn't feel

empty.

WRITER'S BLOCK

The little words that line my page
mock me so for I am stuck
and stuck they are and berate me too
for unfinished they will never feel
complete, whole, satisfied
and neither will I.

HOW TO CATCH A DAYDREAM

As I stare into the void
beyond my laptop's screen
I wonder how I'll go about
catching my daydreams.

I ask myself more frequently
where it is that I might find
all these dizzying faeries
that seem to patrol my mind?

The ones that bounce at the skirts of my eyes
and whisper lightly in my ears
those occasional sweet nothings
that I find I want to hear.

I think they might be good to catch,
who knows what I might learn
from all my twisted wishful thoughts
but to my work I must return.

THIS IS WHERE THE DREAMERS LIVE

Let us drift away, my dear,
hand in hand into the sky
over the clouds, beyond the trees
like wish-filled lanterns in the breeze
that dare to reach the heavens above
and onward to the great unknown,
for this is where the dreamers live,
now let this be what we call home.

TRAIN STATION

around you is a sea so vast
of blank expressions with hollow eyes
like abandoned shells of lost crabs
which remain like stains of past lives.

they leave their souls on entry
and pack away their hearts,
in the tight padlocked suitcases.
which adorn their spiritless bodies.

where emptiness moves with feigned emotions
through halls and open spaces.
a smile deflected with nonchalance
and carries on with its processes.

INVISIBLE

a torture it is, to be invisible.
you're rarely seen, you're rarely heard
your screams fall flat like forgotten pages
and reach as far as a wingless bird.

what happens to invisibility?
and to all those who endure
the lonely nights which scream, torture
my dear there is no cure.

take it from me, advance while you can
for when you get stuck, you truly are
as invisibility becomes impenetrability
and the shadows become guards,
when your secrets become locks
to doors with no keys.

FOLLOWING LOST PAPERS

Some days I wonder what would become of me
if I took to following lost papers
the ones that fly through the bustling streets
without their owners to tie them down
and without their spines to keep them warm.

What magic would I find inscribed
on the leaflets that are no longer leaves
but bluster about of their own accord?
What secrets would be shared with me
if I could only catch one free-floating page?

Maybe I'd find the meaning of life
transcribed by a hand that no longer lives
but claims that all that I would require
is a handful of chocolate and heartful of love
to cast all my doubts aside and set me free.

Maybe then I too would be a free-floating page
once bound to the book of time but now
dances around in the infinite that is
the memories of all those whose lives I've touched
and whose names I still recall.

Maybe they too might wonder what secrets I hold
and think on the many adventures I've had
as I drift about the seas of their lives
tangling and unravelling alongside their souls…
and it is that which makes me immortal.

PURPOSE

Why am I here?
I think as I stroll the streets
of places that once were familiar
but now look like scenes
from someone else's life.

What are my dreams?
I wonder when asked
for it seems that everyone here
has dreams and goals
but not me for I do not know myself.

What am I good at?
I ask but no one can say
for only I can prove
something about this person
I claim to be but do not know
and never have and probably
never will.

Who am I?
I call out in plea, but I fear no voice will answer.

QUESTIONS FROM MY INNER CHILD

Who was it that set out this plan?
Is there someone I can complain to about this
predicament? For it must be a mistake if I haven't
chosen it. Right?

What has possessed people to want such a thing?
We used to have fun–do you remember fun? –as we
would run in the rain and dirty our skin and bask in
the here and now and never the tomorrows and next
years.

When was it decided that I was to grow up?
Did I miss the day that we all decided we weren't
going to play with toys and dream up worlds beyond
this one, in favour of boring black suits and too-tight
ties and hurtful high heels?

Where is the world I once knew?
The one I saw with colourful eyes, with secrets
bursting from every turn? Where is the pirate ship I
made from a box? Where are my puppets made of
socks? Someone must have painted the whole grey
and taken away all of my toys. That someone should
be scolded.

Why do I now have to figure myself out?
I haven't been trained for such a thing, and I don't
want to be either. I'd rather return to the fantasies on
my shelf and the scribbles on the walls then have to
justify a me that other people need to see for censuses
and school boards and workers' logs and other things
that need me neatly wrapped in a number and tied
with a title.

How do I live with myself now?

NEW JOB

My name? I can manage that.
Experience? What kind?
Do you ask if I can handle a computer? How so?
Do you ask if I can write? Write well?
Do you ask if I can speak? Speak what? To whom?

You need someone who is good with people?
I can be good with people…sometimes.
Must I like them? I don't really like people.
You need references? Does my mum count?
You ask a lot. Will I be good enough?
Maybe I'm not cut out for this job.

You like me? That's great!
What will you pay? How long will you ask of me?
Sell my soul? Is your offer good enough?
Maybe it's not cut out for me…

Dear Mr. Job Offer,

I have reviewed your subpar offer on an exorbitant number of hours a week doing things I don't like, never have, and never will. I understand I will be underpaid and undervalued, and possibly have no options of ascending. I am very pleased to say that I am so afraid of chasing my dreams that I accept your terrible offer.

Sincerely,

The slow fizzle of my dying dreams

MOVING

Who knows why I decided to abandon ship, I think as I stare
on, ticket in my hand, suitcase at my side.
Who knows what waits for me across the ocean,
or what kind of person I will be…

The woman to my left reads a magazine with a name
I can't pronounce but know is French. Her hand curls
delicately as she casually flips the pages. Maybe I will
be like her, model-esque, nonchalant, the western
standard of beauty, the redefinition of haute.

Though she is admired by all, she does not smile.
I like to smile.
No, I will not be her.

The man to my right takes calls in Italian and Polish,
but the book at his side is distinctly English. Maybe I
will be a polyglot, a lingual chameleon like him. I will
master the art of speaking and blending seamlessly
into my environment.

But in his hand is a ticket to Spain yet tells his wife he
goes to Prague. He has also mastered lies.
I do not like to lie.
No, I will not be him.

The man at the desk calls out my flight number. I take
my book in hand–the same tattered one I read every
year. I sling my jumper around my hips–the same
comfy one I always wear.

I turn back to the exit–a final goodbye to my old life.
Maybe I will just be me, somewhere else, not
someone else. *Maybe I don't have to decide,*
I think as I board the plane.

IMPOSTOR SYNDROME I

Perfect

I can be that.
I can do that.
I can get there.
I can make it.
If I try.
Harder.
Faster.
Better.
Longer.

If I try, I must get there.
I've done this before.
You know I can, so I must.
Right? Always right,
can never be wrong.
Must be Perfect.

Can't sleep, need time.
Can't eat, not hungry.
Can't stop.
Must be Perfect.

THE WORKER BEE IN ME

the worker bee in me, it buzzes
noisily around my head
breaking any chance i have at peace
and any night's hope of dreamless sleep
leaving a burning in my flustered cheeks
and colouring them stoplight red.

sleep deprived and shivering
i cannot yet sit still
i cry until my heart gives out
until i wish to scream and shout
until a migraine pounds about
and i'm left feeling ill.

the anxiety in me, it forces
and from my life sucks all the fun
you may not sit still, it says
even if you're ill, it says
until you pay the bills, it says
not 'til the work is done.

RESTLESS

how night descends with peaceful breezes
and yet you lie awake
your eyes, they burn, and your tears, they sting
and your heart does none but ache.

when thought doth lead to tremor
and imagination dies
what is left for perfect slumber?
and who to dry your eyes?

rustles from the outside world
are all your ears can hear
when 2 a.m. creeps slowly forward
yet daylight never near.

your mind beats to the ticking clock
how dark this world you've known
becomes with tired eyes and hands
how lonely…how alone.

and though the day may give reprieve
the cycle doth repeat
as restlessness doth eat your centre
'til you beg and plead for sleep…

ICED

Some may argue that this drink is just coffee served cold, but recent history has shown it can be so much more. Between the wide range of beans, roasts, milks, syrups, powders, and serving vessels, this drink is one part coffee, all parts treat.

The beverage is usually prepared using a shot of espresso–though any brew type will do–and flavoured to one's preferences using milks, syrups, or powders. And, of course, served over a few cubes of ice.

The following poems have been served up cold, as per brewing instructions. Some are bitter, others are sweet, and some even contain the slightest flavouring of Christmas. Whether it's a hot summer's day or a cold winter's eve, these poems bring the chill.

SNOWFLAKES

If I were a snowflake, I'd take my time
drifting around in the endless sky
over the spindly hands that once were trees,
leafy and green now barren and grey
reaching up to catch me the way
I catch on children's eyelashes
but I don't stay too long.

If I were a snowflake, I'd wonder about
the world beyond my own icy paradise
about things I could barely imagine
like green grasses and red roses
and places I could never live,
whose salty sands I'll never touch
and humid airs I'll never know.

If I were a snowflake, I'd soar just high enough
to gaze upon the world below
where I could watch some snowflakes settle
while others like me fill the empty skies
to take comfort in our great divides
casually intertwining and sometimes colliding
to remind ourselves we're not alone.

THE FIRST TIME

Seeing you was like seeing snow for the first time.
Spine-tingling, eye-opening.

Blinding, like that first ray of sun that reflects off the
glittering mounds that appeared the night before.

Enchanting, like following a single flake to the ground
as the blizzard picks up behind it.

Slow and fast, and suddenly infinite,
as if time were nothing but an afterthought.

HOLIDAY RUSH

Hang the decorations all over the tree
sweep the needles all up from the floor
set up the lights so they sparkle at night
find a wreath to put over the door.

Buy the sprinkles and sugar for the cookies we'll make
buy the ham and the pot roast and corn
and a box of candy canes just for the sake
and bows for the presents we'll adorn.

The season is here to be cheery again
the season for telling the truth
when new love may flourish, and old love grows on
and joy floods the eyes of the youth.

So, bring in the sparkles, the tinsel and toys
bring in the bells and the boughs
and when you finish with all the hustle and bustle
I'll be waiting for you under the mistletoe.

WHERE DID THE WARMTH GO?

The heater is on, but my hands are cold
they feel like ice beneath my blanket,
I'd put on gloves and a hat and maybe a coat
if only this chill would leave, but it stays.

The house is fine, but my floor is freezing
my feet on the tile feel numb to it,
the windows are shut and the doors are closed
but the frigid air still finds its way in.

There's ice in my chest and it will not budge
from the place where my heart once was,
there's a storm in my soul that batters my bones
and leaves me wondering if I'll ever get warm.

CANDLE

where is the light for which i asked
twenty minutes before?
my heart is cold, my hands are tired
my eyes are growing sore.

where is the light for which i seek
the brilliant, burning flame?
something, please to keep the chill
from finding out my name.

He sits across the table
as His cold hands reach for mine
frost trickles from His fingertips
to me, too much, to Cold: too fine.

candle, come, candle
light's fleeting flickering flame.
trickle soft, but down you trickle
too late. He knows my name.

GROWING COLD

press your face against my cheek
and feel the icy chill
something has come over me
my mind is growing still

run your fingers through my hair
and take my hand in yours
something somewhere seems it's broken
and weary, i grow sore

rest your hand upon my heart
and transfer something warm
lost in streams of awful dreams
my heart strings are left torn

hold your lips against my own
and show me all your love
maybe that will save my soul
maybe that's enough.

ON THE INSIDE LOOKING OUT

"Hello, how are you?"
they ask with a smile.

"I'm fine, and you?" is all they expect
is all you will give, for you expect it too.
but on the inside, you grow cold.

On the inside looking out
you're broken, you're shattered
you cry when no one is looking
because you can't when they're around.
your smiles have grown fake and tiring
but you know no better.

On the inside looking out
your fears surround you
you surrender to the voices inside your head,
each saying something to keep you down,
to keep you at bay,
to keep you submissive.

And no one around you knows.

On the inside, you scream, you scream loudly,
"Help! Help me!"
help me.

On the inside you're dying
though no one can hear
no one will listen.
but would you let them?

On the inside your heart is breaking
and looking out is no better.

On the inside looking out
you're tortured,
you face despair alone
alone, alone.
And no one around you knows.
but will they ever?
no one around you knows any better.

your smile is all they have ever seen
your tears do not exist.
for if they did the world would shatter
and day would turn to mist.

On the inside looking out...
"I'm fine," and walk away.

A DATE WITH DEATH

with his shiny fingertips
and all his icy claws
nothing had I ever seen
none like this at all.

he held me with his blinding gaze
and pearl white frozen smile
and wrapped me in a blanket cold
to keep me for a while.

before I caught a wisp of breath
before the light did fade
he closed my eyes with gentle hands
and to him I obeyed.

a beauty I have never seen
a love so soft and fine
the pull of passion, touching death
as his darkened hands touched mine…

FALLING TO PIECES

a tired old swing, falling to pieces
the chain links broken, the wood is cracked
forgotten it's been–for years it seems–
in the garden, in the back.

and life may touch it–falling to pieces
as back and forth it glides
but falling is falling, and it's falling to pieces
what secrets does it hide?

a pair of lovers sit quietly
one over, one below
the woman hanging in the swing
her lover in the snow

and neither spoke, and neither moved
her dress fell long and black
and dragged across the furtive snow
to graze her lover's back.

his and hers, it was their swing
but now there's no more him
the woman above and the grave below
her light is growing dim.

a tired old swing–falling to pieces
sits quiet with a story to tell
but falling is falling–and it's falling to pieces
and then one day it fell.

BLACK

For those who like their coffee bold and unapologetic, black coffee is the ultimate choice. Made with just coffee and water, it's a straightforward yet powerful drink that's perfect for starting your day or keeping you focused throughout it.

Made in a drip coffee maker or a French press, this drink is perfect for those who crave the bold and robust taste of coffee, without the added sweetness or creaminess of other popular beverages. This brew is a dark, bitter, no-nonsense kind of drink, and with more water comes a deeper mug.

The following poems contain darker, slightly sobering undertones. Like the black coffee, they are long and bitter, and perfect for stormy weather.

IN MEMORIAM

I never knew I'd miss the sea
The salty songs that saunter up
Upon the sparkling sandy shores
But you did.

The way the waves would wash away
The worries of the waking world
But you did.

I never knew I'd miss the breeze
The billowing clouds that bob above
The branches of the bending palms
But you did.

The whistles of the whispering rocks
From where we watched the world go by
But you did.

The chirping chittering chattering
Of the crickets, gulls and clicking crabs
But you did.

I never knew I'd miss the peace
The push and pull of setting suns
And rising moons in open skies
But you did.

The twinkle of the starry seas
Like cities cast below a wing
But you did.

The stillness that lulled our hearts to sleep
On beaches, blissful paradise
Yes, you did.

But did you know that I would miss
The way we used to run and laugh
And toss our troubles to the sea
And sing awake the neighbour's dogs
And swing from frangipani trees
And while away the wading tide
And wish ourselves the King and Queen
Of lands we'd never get to see
When we were nothing more than kids
And you were still alive with me

'Cause I did.
'Cause I still do.
'Cause I always will.

A LIFE IN MEMORY (TO MY GRANDCHILD)

I remember the ocean
the waves upon the shore
the winds rustling through the trees
on the island where I was born.

I remember the first step
I set foot in a school,
as if yesterday I was yay high
and no more than two.

I remember the first wink I was given
the first time I blushed
and how a first love grew
from just a first crush.

I remember the heartache that followed,
the feeling of imperfection
that bubbled and boiled
when looking at my reflection.

I remember the travelling, the joy,
the overwhelming emotion
from the first time I experienced
a city in motion.

I remember my first kiss
and how my heart must have popped
for stop the love did,
but the memory did not.

I remember the first time
I set off on my own
a little bit lonely
and a long way from home.

the first job I got
I remember all too well,
a pretty young waitress
with a story to tell.

I remember the first time we met
I was just shy of nineteen
and he only twenty
in his eyes was our dream

and after years of together
of hoping it was right
he asked me to marry him
and I said I just might.

I remember our wedding
the joy and the tears
the happiness that came
with my father's cheers.

the first house we bought
was not all that great
the doors creaked; the roof leaked
we had a fence with no gate.

I remember our first storm,
oh how the winds they did howl,
and the lightning it struck
and the thunder it growled.

I remember the birth
of our beautiful baby girl
and thinking how we could raise her
in this mess of a world.

we did though my dear
and she turned out just fine,

and she made her own memories
in time, just like mine.

after a while
we began to grow old
something went wrong
or, so I was told.

the first time I saw
my dear husband cry
was when the doc told me
I was going to die.

I had some disease
that eats at the brain,
but he sat there and told me
he loved me the same.

since then, I remember
it was him who went first,
a car accident struck
I still picture the hearse.

from that day I remember
things weren't quite the same
my symptoms had worsened
I lost track of his name

these days I'm alone, child,
all I'm hearing are lies
from people who speak well of me
with tears in their eyes.

the doctors can't fix me
no cure can they find
but my incurable disease isn't Alzheimer's
…it's time.

NOT TODAY

Today the rain falls from wet cheeks to dry streets
Today the blue skies are more blue
Today the wind howls, and in it your name,
so not even black coats will keep out its chill.

Today the sun's rays do not keep their promise
Today their yellow shines grey
Today the clouds hide their silver linings
for not even they can find reason to hope.

Today the world turns, but I am stuck here
watching the face of the one I once loved
still and pale and resting, they say
but I shall not rest tonight.

NOT EVEN SOUR MILK

Not even sour milk is worse
than the taste of longing on my lips
that spoils the things I once enjoyed
but haven't since you passed.

Without you here nothing tastes right
even sweet chocolate tastes bland
to this pain and longing no foul taste compares
not even sour milk.

WAIT FOR ME

I know you must be busy
and I hope you're having fun
doing all the things that you once loved
and all the things you'd never tried
and wanted to but never could.

I know you must be occupied
by the many long-lost relatives
that must be swarming to greet you there
and tell you their lives' stories
having watched over you and yours.

But schedule me in if there's still space
for the person you once loved but left
too soon and too heartbroken on
this heavy patch of earthly life
that no longer holds you captive.

It would mean this world to me
and–of course– the one beyond
if you still remembered me and
the promise you made with your final breath
that you'd wait for me up there.

HALF EMPTY CUP

silence the messages
turn off my phone
shut all the doors
pretend i'm not home

my clocks have all stopped
my roses turned black
i still wait up all night
hoping you will come back

your last cup of coffee
sits half drunk and all cold
on the table in the house
where we'd planned to grow old

all the well-wishers
come bowing their heads
with promises of better
saying don't pity the dead

but the mourners have left now
and with no clouds in the skies
the rain, it still pours down
in streams from my eyes

maybe i'll find you
in another life, my friend
where we'll be a different boy and a different girl
with different stories and a better end.

THE THINGS YOU LEAVE BEHIND

all the things you leave behind
are never cut in stone.
they are all the dreams and all the loves
and all the places you called home.

they are all the peaceful slumbers
and all the restless nights
they are all the open-ended talks
and all the unfinished fights.

they are all places we'll never go to
and all the adventures we'll never have
they are all the kisses and all the hugs
and all the tears and laughs.

all the things you leave behind
feel broken when you're gone
too many things were left unsaid
too many left undone.

ESPRESSO

A full-flavoured, concentrated shot of coffee, made with finely ground beans and pressurized, steaming hot water, this is the base of all coffee beverages. Can be identified by its small size and layering of *crema* created when the steam hits the natural oils of the coffee.

The following poems capture the essence of the espresso, packing a lot of punch into a few lines. Like their coffee counterpart, these poems are highly concentrated and strong, with mixed undertones. Great for a quick pick-me-up or a sobering dose of reality.

MY SILENT CRIES

my silent cries are never seen
nor ever heard or shown
but they are there, for i can hear
and i know they are my own.

i hold it in with all my might
and try to hide my frown
but when i reach my house at night
i seem to just break down.

though i do not cry aloud
and none know what i think
these thoughts appear despite the crowd
and in class a tear smudges my ink.

LOOK ME IN THE EYES, MY LOVE

We board up our souls and lock up our hearts
and blind our eyes to tragedy
longing is lost, and emotions flee
as not in the eyes do you look at me.

But if you don't look into my eyes
how then will I see your heart?
For love today is all but truth,
it is a mastery—a mere art.

THE SINS OF TIME

Time is just a bastard
who looks to torture all
by turning moments to remember
into those we don't recall

Time is just a bastard
to give reason to our age
to poison all that we have wanted
and to whom we must obey

Time is just a bastard
He watches as we live
and controls our fate and kills our hope
with nothing more to give

Time is just a bastard
the product of vanity
to Him we think our lives live on
we think that He can see

Time is just a bastard
who sits and mocks us all
turning moments to remember
into ones no one recalls.

HERE I AM, YOUR BROKEN CLOCK

here i am, your Broken clock
the one that can't tell time
the one you've left to catch the dust
and the dreams you left behind

here i am, your Broken clock
the one that doesn't ring
my clockwork's busted, a chain is loose
and now i no longer sing

here i am, your Broken clock
the one that used to tick
but something's jammed in my insides
and now i only stick

here i am, your Broken clock
the one that fell quite hard
when the ground beneath my feet felt faint
now my face is none but shards

here i am, Your broken clock
the one You don't recall
the one that sits on some old shelf
with its face against the wall.

IMPOSTOR SYNDROME II

there is no way
I will not
I cannot
I do not
don't you see?

I was not who
I needed
Me to be
I never was
for who is She?

the many lies
I told Myself
to get Me through the day
have left Me

weary, withered
with bitter thoughts
and tired hands
product of vanity
creature of insanity

plagued by voices
in My head
that claim to Me
that I am and can be
that which only breaks Me more

and still, I ~~try~~ die to please.

THERE IS A GAP INSIDE MY SOUL

there is a gap inside my soul
a gap that can't be filled
and much to all my failed patches
it grows wider, wider still.

there is a gap inside my soul
a gap from all the pain
a gap from all the loss I've known
a gap from all the shame.

there is a wound under my skin
that cannot be repaired
a wound that leaves me tortured, scratching
that leaves me in despair.

there is a hole inside my heart
for which there is no cure
and many nights I wake in tears
of that I can be sure.

there is a gap inside my soul
and the gap becomes a void
when dawns the brash and shocking truth
I was nothing but a toy.

VICTIMS

We were both victims of our egos,
unwilling to see the pain of the other
as pain taped our own eyes shut
and left our open wounds to fester.

THE COUNTDOWN

it took years to find something
that took months to blossom
that which more months would soil and wither
until the days fell like leaves untethered
down to the minutes before
the second it snapped.

L. M. SANGUINETTE

THE HATE BUSH

in my own pain I couldn't see
the damage I was leaving behind
the seeds of hatred I was sowing
fed only with salty tears and sour words
whose swollen tender roots grew
forever downwards
taking with them my broken heart.

tender roots that must be broken
as does this ego that has outgrown me
and replaced with something that
sprouts flowers above instead of thorns.

WRITING ON THE WALL

This house feels like a shell,
something hollow, something cold
and where I try to fill it,
with things that feel like me
posters, pictures, paintings, pity
I find that nothing sticks.

I replace the posters on the wall
time and time again and still
each time they fall they take pieces of me,
plucked remains, until I am something
less than whole and realize that
it's me that doesn't stick.

CAFÉ BOMBON

Comprised of equal parts espresso and condensed milk, this traditional Spanish coffee beverage contains a flavour profile reminiscent of caramel and serves as the final drop of bittersweet reflection needed to close this tale.

The poems in this section are just as rich and indulgent as the Cafe Bombon itself. They explore themes of sweetness and indulgence, while also touching on the more bittersweet aspects of life. The warm and comforting tones of these poems make them perfect for a cozy night in, curled up with a cup of this sweet and creamy beverage.

PATHS

I walked ahead only to find
the path I'd already travelled upon.
So, I closed my eyes and walked behind,
hoping to find a different one.

REACHING OUT IN THE DARK

Give me your hand
and I'll help you cross
the bridges of our secret lives
and chasms of our darkest minds
safe from the many jagged claws
of our ill-wishing anxieties
and all of their disciples.

SHOOTING STARS

I make a wish on falling stars
to keep the magic alive.
For someone must
if the rest of the grownups
have decided to leave it behind.
And I think I see
at the other end
of the blinding tail of light
a glimmer of hope
with a hint of mystique
which will get me through the night.

LOST IN THE NIGHT

the night is a mystifying thing.
it removes all traces of colour,
all blemishes, all marks
to it we are all equal,
passersby waiting
if only for the break
of the new day.

but in it there's magic.
in the darkest of the night
that adds the illusion of perfection
to each and every imperfection
and whatever's lost
in the cracks between
is made up for with
imagination.

STARGAZING

The stars above tell stories,
says my mother to me
say I to my daughter dearest
and her to her daughters three.

The stars above give meaning to
our little lives below
as we stare up, so they stare back
and show us where to go.

The stars above remind us all
how small we truly are
but find beauty in our little lives
when shared with those both near and far.

ROSE PETAL HEART

When the shattered pieces of my heart
fell like petals from a rose's stem
I softly resigned to my darker fate
thinking that would be the end.

But then you came and picked them up
gently and one by one
bound them in a book with care
'til I became something new
but I was whole again.

YOU ARE STRONG MY DARLING

You may not see it now My Darling,
but you are stronger than you know.
Once you've cried the tears you cry,
once your fears no longer hide
you will see what I can see,
the you I know you're meant to be
not that which shies away from all
but that doesn't break despite a fall
like the sturdy oak the wind can't blow
My Darling, you are strong.

THE GETTING BETTER

I promise you it all gets better,
every rough patch and sleepless night
every broken heart and shattered bone
every missing thing and every missing one,
it will all get better one day.

This is not the easy part, but you will learn to grow
and all the things that hurt you once
will tie you down no longer
when you learn that all it takes to be free
is getting through the getting better.

WHERE DO THE DAYS GO?

Where do all the days go?
The good ones and the bad?
The ones I spent down by the seaside
chasing seagulls up the sand?

And what about the ones I spent
listening to your laugh
as we stared up at the fluffy clouds
watching as they passed?

How about the lonely ones
I spent all by myself?
The ones I spent at the foot of my bed
praying for someone's help?

What about the icky ones
from all the times I felt ill?
And all the lazy ones in which
I wanted just to chill?

Where are all the teary ones?
The scaredy-cat ones too?
And the lovey-dovey dreamy ones
that I spent thinking of you?

Where do all the days go
that I thought were not the best?
They may not have been perfect,
but I love them like the rest.

Where do all the days go
when you finally reach the end?
I hope they're kept in somewhere safe
the good, the bad, the not so great
stored on a magical memory tape
so I can live them again.

US

There's something about the way we fit
that no one can quite comprehend
like streaks of gold through walls of stone
perfectly inlaid and complementary
whereby whatever gaps I have you fill
and whatever bonds you have I strengthen.

KISS ME SLOWLY

A simple kiss from you feels like
a thousand tiny suns
sparkling through my streaming blood
sending a blaze through my every cell
and as I blush, I glow
like every star that beams above
in the darkest of the night's skies
captured and placed
into the little jar I call my body
that you now hold firmly
as you draw yourself in closer
until our breaths are sharing breaths
and our hearts beat as one
filling the space between us with
an expectant passion that keeps us tangled
blurring the lines that define
where you end and I begin
and you lean in again to kiss me
slowly.

L. M. SANGUINETTE

DANCING AS WE FALL IN LOVE

If this were all a book, my dear
I'd write it so we fell in love.
The kind of love that leaves us dancing
on the busy, bustling city streets,
open and exposed for all to see,
drawing the crowd in close around,
but you'd twirl me in despite their gaze
and in your arms we'd both agree
to dance like no one is watching.

COUNTING THE FIREFLIES

Whoever'd told me, long ago
that I'd be here with you beneath
the open canvas of starry skies
counting the blinking fireflies,
I might not have believed them then
for the you I knew before all this
was not someone I would've spent
my time with watching fireflies fly
in circles 'round our dreamy heads,
but I'll swallow the pride I wore like a badge
and admit that I was wrong.

CHANGE

They said I'd never learn to change
that my stubbornness would not budge
that I couldn't learn to be anything but
the only person they wanted to see
thereby keeping me in my place.

But I chose to change the way I thought
of how they thought about me and saw
that only I could choose whether or not
I was allowed to change and so
I did, and now I'm free.

IMPOSTOR SYNDROME III

it is my ego
and mine alone
that requires of me
this lack of sleep
to turn the little good in my life
into something great
that my inner self
does not want
but has been convinced
it needs.

now i alone
must forge ahead
forgetting all
that once was taught
that once was learned
that once was expected
to find the me i truly am
and the one i want
to be.

UNLEARNING TO LOVE (DEAR MR)

Dear mr,
Excuse me as I unlearn to love
the way I was taught,
the way I had seen,
the way I was shown.
I am unlearning to fear it
unlearning worry, unlearning pain.

Unlearning that which said
my love was not good enough,
those fears that held me,
that said you would leave
that said I would break
that said my love was broken,
that I was, but now I know better.

Now I know these are only
the demons in my mind
and I now see that these
do not control as they think they do
not me, not you, not us.

Now I'm learning to love again
to trust again, to believe again
so I can love you truly
and I can love me newly
to be there for you for worse or better
because I promised you forever.

THE DAY I FELL

I still remember the day I fell
the shattering of something deep
hidden away from all of me
so that when it shattered it tore
through mind and matter and ideas
I hadn't realized I had
of things I thought I might have been
if I were someone different
or I were something more.

But the broken pieces glistened
like the first drops of rain
after the drought that caused the life in me
to dry and crumble like the barren lands
we leave behind in favour of
greener plains and brighter skies.

I realized then that there was no drought,
that I was not barren or broken
that all my little pieces became
little flecks of gold spread wide
glittering in streams for panners to find
and I had become something new
something more than I ever would've
before the day I fell.

THIS DAY IS FOR COFFEE (REPRISED)

this day was for coffee,
for silent thoughts to share,
for angsty teenage ponderings
for feelings all laid bare.

this day was for coffee,
for new smiles and old friends,
for all the teary sweet goodbyes
and all the bitter ends.

this day was for coffee,
for walks down memory lane,
for capsuled thoughts and fantasies,
for gentle lovers' pain.

this day was for coffee,
for strangers newly met,
and yes, it's true, the day is done,
but reader, don't you fret,

for this day was for coffee,
though yesterday was for tea
tomorrow still has yet to come
who knows what it will be...

OTHER WORKS IN THIS COLLECTION...

If you enjoyed this book, please feel free to leave a review of it on your favourite sites. These reviews help small-time authors like me reach new audiences and are much appreciated!

Stay up to date on L. M. Sanguinette's new releases and giveaways by signing up for her mailing list or following her on social media. Find all the links at the page below:

https://linktr.ee/lmsanguinette/

Be on the lookout for more books coming soon!

ABOUT THE AUTHOR

L. M. Sanguinette was born on a small island in the Caribbean, where the palm trees watched over her like giants and the sea crept up to her feet to say hello. Ever since she was little, she surrounded herself with tales of fantasy and magic, hoping that one day, she too would be involved in a story like the ones that captured her imagination.

Years—and many rewatching's of Avatar the Last Airbender—later, she is happily living in the worlds that her mind created, filling her bookshelves with more books than she will ever read, and practising her own version of magic.

When she's not sitting at the computer, she can be found snorkelling near forgotten shores, twisting from silks that hang from the ceilings, or in one of the many hidden coffee shops of Madrid, conversing with the spirits of the old city and dreaming up new adventures.

OTHER WORKS

Welcome to Visanthe (#1, Legend of the Stones)
Visanthe in Ruin (#2, Legend of the Stones)
Visanthe Rising (#3, Legend of the Stones)

Of Arrows and Roses

The Days I Dream of Coffee
The Days I Dream of Chocolate
The Days I Dream of Chardonnay

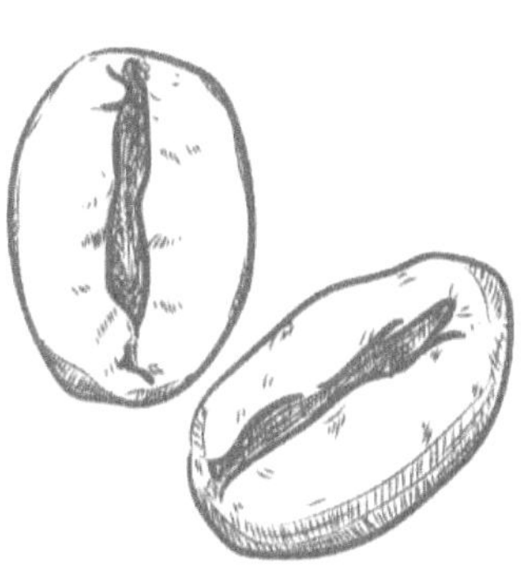